MATHS PLUS
FROM HEINEMANN

Maths Games

R

Teacher's Notes

Heinemann

Heinemann Educational
a division of Heinemann Publishers (Oxford) Ltd
Halley Court, Jordan Hill, Oxford OX2 8EJ

OXFORD LONDON EDINBURGH
MADRID ATHENS BOLOGNA PARIS
MELBOURNE SYDNEY AUCKLAND SINGAPORE TOKYO
IBADAN NAIROBI HARARE GABORONE
PORTSMOUTH NH (USA)

© Margo Fourman 1996
First published 1996
Designed and illustrated by Small House Design

Printed in Great Britain
Illustrated by Cathy Baxter, Lynne Farmer, Helen Floate, Stuart Trotter

ISBN 0435 02356 X   (Games box and Teacher's Notes)
    0435 02366 7   (Teacher's Notes only)

Contents

Introduction   1

Teddy Bears' Picnic   3

Sea Rescue   5

Ducklings   7

Caterpillar, Caterpillar   9

Splash!   11

Treasure   14

Puffa Train   17

Teddy Allsorts   19

Introduction

Purpose of the games

'Maths Games' is a series of games packs to supplement mathematics teaching in the primary school. In Maths Games R, for the Reception and Nursery class, we have aimed to provide:

○ well illustrated, attractive materials which will capture and hold the interest of this age group

○ motivating situations in which new ideas and concepts are presented in a meaningful way

○ opportunities to practise newly acquired skills and build confidence and competence.

In addition, the games support learning and supplement any mathematics programme by:

○ providing a focus for mathematical talk, questions and answers which develop and clarify the children's ideas

○ sustaining the children's interest and gradually increasing their attention spans

○ being used in conjunction with illustrations and materials which enable children to check calculations and decisions.

Mathematical coverage

The overall content of Maths Games R relates to Level 1 of the National Curriculum and the Northern Ireland curriculum, and Level A of Mathematics 5–14 (Scotland).

The main focus of the games is one-to-one matching; number recognition and counting to 6; sorting and sequencing. Since all the games involve an element of Using and Applying Mathematics, this aspect of the curriculum is not emphasised specifically in the curriculum references.

References to the curriculum

The maths content of the games will form a useful introduction to the concepts developed in the relevant curriculum for each country. References are therefore included for each game. These relate to the Key Stage 1 programme of study, Level 1 (for England and Wales, and Northern Ireland) and to Level A (for Scotland). For example, the main focus for Teddy Bears' Picnic (page 3) is indicated by the following reference:

England and Wales
Number, subsection 2a

N2a

Scotland
Range and Type of Numbers

RTN

Northern Ireland
Number, Understanding number
and number notation, part a

NUa

The **While the children are playing. . .** section draws attention to possible responses from the children.

Support for good primary practice

The games provide meaningful tasks in an atmosphere of achievement and success. They also provide opportunities for:

challenge

Children are encouraged to think for themselves and show what they can do. The games give choices, reward planning ahead and encourage simple strategies.

differentiation

Some children need to take smaller steps towards understanding than others. Each of the games has suggestions for simpler versions. The basic materials may be adapted to meet varying needs. Extension activities suggest ways of developing the activity for more able children.

enjoyment

All the games have been trialled to ensure 'repeat playability'. Children will be able to practise the same skill repeatedly while continuing to enjoy the game.

independent working

Initially, an adult is needed to establish the rules and context. Children usually find it easy to take over responsibility for the games because the story or situation makes a logical sequence. Simplified photocopiable rules for each game are provided at the end of the notes for that game.

building confidence

Children gain confidence in their own ability to learn so that mathematics is not a guessing game. The games are designed to enable children to check their own decisions and calculations through using apparatus or illustrations.

learning from each other

The games encourage children to co-operate by explaining rules and checking each other's work.

parental involvement

The photocopiable version of the rules may easily be passed to an adult helper in the classroom, or sent home with a child for parental involvement.

Teddy Bears' Picnic

a game for 2–3 players, taking 15 minutes

Purpose

○ practises counting to 3

○ practises one to one correspondence

Materials needed

provided in the pack
Teddy Bears' Picnic playing board
I counter for each player

also needed
3 coins
3 spare coins (Extension)

Introducing the game

The teddy bears are having a picnic by the river. To join in the picnic, players need to cross the river using the stepping stones. Throw the coins to show you how many steps to take. You may take one step for each face showing on the coins. Who will get to the picnic first?

How to play

1 All the players put their counters on Start.
2 The first player throws 3 coins and counts the faces showing.
3 They move that number of steps across the river.
4 If no faces show, they sing 'Zero, zero, have another go', and throw again.
5 They pass the coins to the next player.
6 When they reach the other bank they can go to the teddy bears' picnic.
7 The first player to get to the picnic is the winner.

> Zero, zero, have another go.

Making the game easier
Take turns to throw the coins, but all players move the same counter. This makes a quick game for children with a short attention span and no one has to worry about losing.

Extensions
Extra turns: Add another rule—if all 3 coins land face up, players may have another turn.
Higher numbers: Use 4, 5 or 6 coins to extend the counting required.

While the children are playing . . .

Can the child count the faces accurately every time?
Can they move the right number of steps without help?

Teddy Bears' Picnic

a game for 2–3 players

You will need

Teddy Bears' Picnic playing board
3 coins
1 counter each

How to play

1 Take 1 counter each and put them on Start.

2 In your turn, throw 3 coins and count the number of faces showing.

3 Move your counter that number of steps across the river.

4 If no faces show, sing 'Zero, zero, have another go', and throw the coins again.

5 The winner is the first player to get to the picnic.

Sea Rescue

a game for 2–4 players, taking about 10 minutes

Purpose

○ practises counting to 3

○ teaches and practises comparative language

Materials needed

provided in the pack
Sea Rescue playing board
24 fish
1 counter for each player

also needed
3 coins
1–6 spot dice (Extension)

Introducing the game

A tanker has spilled oil into the sea and the fish are in danger. The mermaids want you to help them to save the fish. There are some pools of clean water here for the fish to live in. It is your job to take the fish out of the sea one at a time and put them in your clean pool.

How to play

1 Each player puts their counter on Start.
2 Players put the fish in the sea in the centre of the board and find the pool which matches the colour of their counter, to put their fish in.
3 The first player throws 3 coins and counts the faces.
4 They move one space forward for each face showing.
5 If no faces show they sing 'Zero, zero, have another go', and throw again.
6 If they land on a fish, they pick up a fish from the sea and put it in their pool.
7 Continue until all the fish have been saved.
8 The winner is the player with the most fish in their pool.

Making the game easier
Take turns to throw the coins, but all players move the same counter and put the fish into the same pool. Continue until all the fish have been saved.
This makes a quick game for children with a short attention span: there are no winners or losers.

Extension
Higher numbers: Use a 1–6 spot dice to extend number recognition and counting.

While the children are playing . . .

Does the child count the number of faces accurately every time?
Does the child recognise 1, 2 or 3 faces without touching and counting the coins?
Does the child move the right number of spaces without help?
Can they compare the numbers of fish they have saved using appropriate vocabulary? (ie 'more', 'one more', 'fewer', 'equal', 'the same')

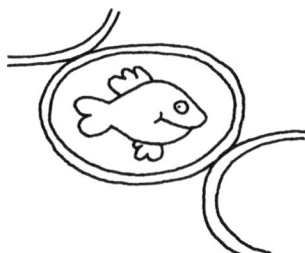

If I land on a fish, I can save a fish from the sea

Sea Rescue

a game for 2–4 players

You will need

Sea Rescue playing board
3 coins
24 fish
1 counter each

How to play

1 Take 1 counter each and put them all on Start.

2 Put the fish in the sea and find a pool which matches the colour of your counter.

3 In your turn, throw 3 coins and count the number of faces showing.

4 Move your counter that number of spaces.

5 If no faces show, sing 'Zero, zero, have another go', and throw the coins again.

6 If you land on a fish, take a fish from the sea and put it in your pool.

7 Give the coins to the next player.

8 Go on until all the fish have been saved.

9 Count the number of fish you have saved. Who has the most? That person is the winner.

Ducklings

a game for 3-4 players, taking 10-15 minutes

Purpose

○ practises one to one correspondence

○ practises number recognition to 5 including zero

○ practises counting to 5

N 2a

RTN

NUab

Materials needed

provided in the pack
4 Ducklings playing boards
counters to cover ducklings (15 each)
1 pack of 24 0–5 number cards

Introducing the game

Look at the playing boards, talk about eggs and hatching. Players cover each baby duckling with a counter. We are pretending that the counters are the shells of the eggs. We will have to wait for the ducklings to hatch. They will hatch when they are ready.

How to play

1 Everyone covers all the ducklings on their board with counters.
2 The 0–5 number cards are put in a pile in the middle face down.
3 Players take it in turns to pick up a card.
4 They say the number and take off the correct number of counters.
  Those ducklings have hatched.
5 If players turn over a zero card, no counters are taken away.
6 The card is returned to the bottom of the pack.
7 The winner is the first person to hatch all their eggs.

Making the game easier
Play with two children, using 1 playing board and 6 numeral cards—
one each of 0–5. Take turns to take a card, say the number and take off the counters.
This is a quick game with no winners or losers.

Extension
Adding eggs: Make a pack of 6–8 number cards and use these to extend the range of the counting required.

While the children are playing . . .

Does the child recognise the numbers on the cards instantly?
Does the child count the eggs accurately?

I have hatched 2 ducklings

Ducklings

a game for 2–4 players

You will need

1 Ducklings playing board each
24 0–5 cards
Counters to cover ducklings (15 each)

How to play

1 Cover all the ducklings on your board with counters.

2 Put the 0–5 number cards face down in a pile in the middle.

3 In your turn, take a card.

4 Take off the correct number of counters. That number of ducklings have hatched.

5 If you turn over a zero card, you cannot take off any counters.

6 The winner is the first person to hatch all their eggs.

Caterpillar, Caterpillar

a game for 2–4 players, taking 10–20 minutes

N2a

RTN

NUab

Purpose

○ practises recognition of numerals and amounts 1–6

Materials needed

provided in the pack
24 Caterpillar cards
1–6 numeral dice

1–6 spot dice (Making the game easier)
1–3 spot dice (Making the game easier)

Introducing the game

Look at the cards with the children. Let them talk about what they can see on both sides. Notice that the numerals match the number of caterpillars. Notice that the holes in the leaf match the numeral on the other side.

How to play

1 Players put all the cards on the table leaf side up.
2 They take turns to throw the numeral dice.
3 Players find a card with the number of holes that matches the number on the dice.
4 They turn the card over to check if the numerals match. If they are right they keep the card. Play continues until there is only 1 caterpillar card left.
5 The winner is the player with the most caterpillar cards.

Making the game easier
Match the numerals: Players place the cards numeral side up and throw the numeral dice. They pick up a card with the same numeral on it.
Match the numbers: Players place the cards leaf side up and throw a 1–6 spot dice. They count the spots on the dice. They find a leaf with the same number of holes.
1,2,3: Use only cards with the numbers 1–3, and use a dice with 1–3 spots.

Extensions
Snap (to encourage quick reactions): Two children share the cards out between them, shuffled so that their sides are mixed up. They take turns to put down a card. If numerals/number of holes match, the first child to say 'Snap' picks up all the cards on the table. Continue until one child has all the cards, or at any time decide who has won by comparing packs: the player with the bigger pack is the winner.
Collect a set: Play as for the original game but players put their number cards in order as they win them. The first player to collect one each of numbers 1 to 6 is the winner.

While the children are playing . . .

Does the child recognise the numeral and say it immediately?
Do they find the right leaf card easily?
Do they always count the holes, even two and three?
Do they recognise some amounts without counting?

This card matches the number on the dice

Caterpillar, Caterpillar

a game for 2–4 players

You will need

24 Caterpillar cards
1–6 numeral dice

How to play

1 Spread the caterpillar cards out on the floor or on the table, leaf sides showing.

2 In your turn, throw the dice and say the number on top.

3 Find a card with that number of holes in the leaf.

4 To check if you are right, turn over the card.

5 If the number is the same as the number on the dice, keep the card.

6 Carry on playing until there is only 1 caterpillar card left.

7 The winner is the person with the most caterpillar cards.

Splash!

a game for 3–4 players, taking 15–20 minutes

Purpose

○ practises counting to 6

○ encourages development of strategy

○ encourages children to explain their thinking

○ reinforces colour recognition

N2a; UA1b, 2c

RTN PSE

NUab

Materials needed

provided in the pack
Splash! playing board
3 counters for each player
1–6 spot dice

1–3 spot dice (Making the game easier)

Introducing the game

Look at the playing board and talk about water slides. Notice that the colours on the track match the colours on the slide and the colours of the counters. Explain that they are going to take turns to move along the track. They can only slide down the slide if they land on their own colour.

How to play

1 Each player takes 3 counters of the same colour and puts them on Start.
2 Players take it in turns to throw the dice.
3 They move 1 of their counters the number of steps shown on the dice.
4 If they land on their own colour, they say 'Wheeee, splash!' then slide down and splash into the pool. Stack these counters on the lilo.
5 They can choose which of their counters to move, but they must move one of them. They cannot move backwards. If they reach the end without landing on their colour, then they go round to Start again.
6 The winner is the first player to get all their counters down the slide and into the splash pool.

I've landed on my colour! Wheeee! Splash!

Making the game easier

One at a time: Use 1 counter at a time. Children take a new counter when one goes down the slide. This removes the decision-making aspect of the game.

1,2,3: Play the game as in the original but use a 1–3 spot dice.

Extensions

Think first: Players must decide which counter to move before they pick one up. Once they have begun to move a counter that has to be their move. This encourages children to look at the alternatives without physically trying out each one.

Two each: Two players can use all the counters and have two colours each. This makes more moves possible and requires the child to think about more alternatives.

While the children are playing . . .

Can the child recognise the number on the dice and move accordingly?

Does the child realise that they have a choice and there is an advantage in checking alternative moves?

Can the child make decisions and explain them?

Does the child plan moves?

Can the child remember and recognise their own colour?

Splash!

a game for 3–4 players

You will need

Splash! playing board
3 counters each
1–6 spot dice

How to play

1 Put your 3 counters (all the same colour) on Start.

2 In your turn, throw the dice and move one of your counters along the top of the slide.

3 If you land on your own colour say 'Wheeee, splash!' and slide your counter down the slide into the splash pool. Then save it on the lilo.

4 After each throw decide which of your 3 counters to move.

5 You must move one of your counters and you cannot move backwards. If you reach the end without landing on your colour you must go back to Start.

6 The winner is the first player to slide all 3 counters into the splash pool.

Treasure

a game for 2–4 players, taking 15–20 minutes

Purpose

○ practises counting to 6

○ reinforces conservation of number

○ introduces the concept of a missing number

○ practises number bonds to 3

N2a, 3c

RTN AS FE

NUab, Oac

Materials needed

provided in the pack
Treasure playing board
1 counter for each player
counters for jewels
1–6 spot dice

Introducing the game

Explain that some dragons are guarding a chest full of treasure. Players are to move along a path, visiting dragons on the way. The dragons like playing tricks. When a player lands on a dragon they will have to work out a puzzle. If the player gets it right, the dragon will give them some treasure.

How to play

1 Each player puts their counter on Start.
2 Players take it in turns to throw the dice.
3 If they land on a dragon they can try to win treasure. An adult or another player puts 3 jewels on the treasure chest. The player closes their eyes. The adult then pretends to be the dragon, and hides some of the jewels under their hand.
4 The player opens their eyes and tries to guess how many jewels are hidden. If the player is right they keep all the jewels from the chest, and 3 more jewels are put in the chest for the next player who lands on a dragon.
5 If their guess is wrong, players have to leave all the jewels in the chest, and no more are added.
6 The winner is the player with the most jewels when everyone gets back to Start.

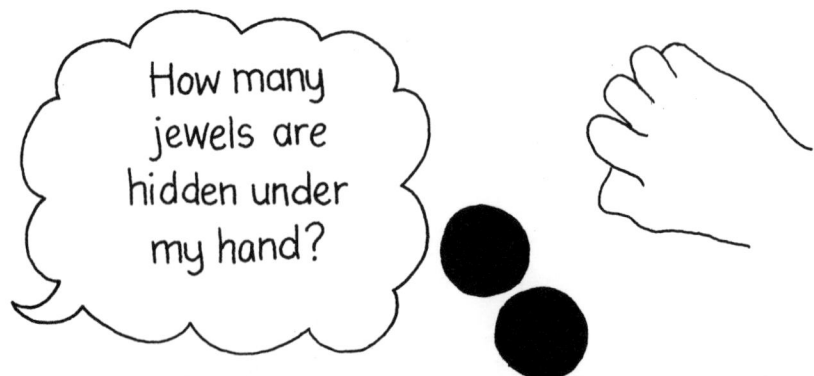

> How many jewels are hidden under my hand?

Making the game easier
Use only 1 counter. Players take turns to throw the dice and move the same counter around the track. When the counter lands on a dragon, an adult hides some of the jewels under their hand. The players decide together how many are missing. This takes the pressure off self-conscious children who are unsure of the answer and afraid of being wrong. Count how many jewels the team have collected when they get back to Start.

Extensions

Higher numbers: Use 4, 5 or 6 jewels and play the original game.

Adding and comparing: The 'dragon' places two sets of jewels on the board and asks 'How many all together?' or 'Which set has more?' or 'Which set has fewer?' (Do not allow the 'dragon' to use more than six counters all together.) If the player is correct, all the counters are kept.

Money: Use 1p and 2p coins for treasure. Place three or four coins in the middle of the board. The dragon hides some of them and asks 'How much money is missing?'

While the children are playing . . .

Does the child guess how many jewels are hidden or do they know?

Are the guesses reasonable? (ie less than the total)

Can the child explain how they know?

Treasure

a game for 2–4 players

You will need

Treasure playing board
1 counter each
counters for jewels
1–6 spot dice

How to play

1 Each person takes 1 counter and puts it on Start.

2 Three jewels are put on the treasure chest.

3 In your turn, throw the dice and move that number of spaces.

4 If you land on a dragon, you must close your eyes.

5 An adult or another player hides some of the jewels under their hand.

6 Open your eyes and say how many jewels are hidden.

7 If you are right you keep all 3 jewels and 3 new ones are put in the middle.

8 If you are wrong you leave the jewels in the middle.

9 When you have all got back to Start, count your jewels. The person with the most jewels is the winner.

Puffa Train

a game for 2–4 players, taking 10 minutes

Purpose

○ practises using ordinal numbers

SSM3a

PM

NUa

Materials needed

provided in the pack
2 train cards for each player
12 tickets
6 counters for each player (as passengers)

12 counters for each player (Extension)

Introducing the game

Look at the trains. Which is the front of the train? Which is the first carriage? Which is the second? Which is the third? Count 6 passengers (use counters, animals or figures). How could they be spaced out in the trains? Explain that in these trains only 1 passenger can go in each carriage. Players are to take tickets to tell them which carriages to put the passengers in.

How to play

1 Players take 2 train cards each. The 12 tickets are placed face down in a pile.
2 They take it in turns to pick up a ticket and read it.
3 Players put a passenger in the carriage shown on the ticket, and replace the ticket at the bottom of the pile.
4 If they already have someone in a carriage in one of their trains, then they can put them in the other train. If both trains have that carriage full, they must replace the ticket at the bottom of the pile and miss that turn.
5 The winner is the first player to put a passenger in each carriage in both trains.

Making the game easier
Two children play co-operatively. Have 1 train in front of the players. Take turns to take a ticket and place a passenger in the right carriage. Instead of replacing the ticket, the player keeps it. This time there is room for 4 passengers in each carriage, so players are sure to be able to place a passenger each time. Go on playing until there are no more tickets in the pile. At the end of the game match the tickets to the passengers in each carriage.

Extension
4th, 5th, 6th: Make additional cards labelled 4th, 5th and 6th. Have 12 counters or other passengers available for each player. Place 2 trains in a line. Explain that there can be 2 passengers in each carriage this time. Play as in the original game, placing passengers correctly in the 1st to the 6th carriages.

While the children are playing . . .

Does the child recognise and say 'first, second', etc, not 'one, two'?
Can the child decide which carriage is first, etc, without help or prompting?

Puffa Train

a game for 2–4 players

You will need

2 train cards each
6 passengers (counters, or small figures)
12 tickets

How to play

1 In your turn, take a ticket from the pile and read it. Put a passenger in that carriage on your first train.

2 Put the ticket back on the bottom of the pile.

3 If you already have a passenger in the carriage on your first train, put the counter on the other train in the correct carriage.

4 If you have passengers in that carriage on both trains, you have to miss that go.

5 The winner is the first person to put a passenger in each carriage of both trains.

Teddy Allsorts

a game for 2–3 players, taking about 10 minutes

Purpose

- ○ compares pictures and notices similarities and differences
- ○ defines and applies sorting criteria
- ○ provides opportunities for children to explain their thinking

N5a; UA3c
O
HDa

Materials needed

provided in the pack
16 bear cards

Introducing the game

Look at the picture cards and talk about the bears. Ask the children to describe a bear each. What colour fur has it? Is it a large bear or a small bear? Is it shaggy or smooth? Has it got trousers on? Is it sitting or standing?

How to play

1 Players spread out all the bear cards face up on the table.
2 In their turns, players choose two cards and say what is the same about them, for example, 'Both these bears have long hair.'
3 The player keeps the pair if the description is correct.
4 If the player is not correct, the cards are replaced on the table.
5 If a player thinks of a category other than those suggested by the illustrations they may keep the cards, for example a child might say 'These bears are like two bears I have at home.'
6 Players continue taking turns to make pairs until all the cards have been picked up.
7 The winner is the player with most bears at the end of the game.

Making the game easier
The teacher specifies the categories, and the children sort into named sets: eg big bears, small bears; bears with bow ties, bears without bow ties; bears sitting down, bears standing up, etc.

Extensions
Bear dominoes: One child chooses any bear card to begin. The next child finds a bear which has at least one factor in common with the first bear, eg a big brown bear with long trousers and a big blond bear with long trousers. The cards are placed end to end. The next player finds another bear in the same way, and places their card next to the second card. Continue around the group, each player saying what has been changed.
Two factors: Play as for the original game, but pick up 2 cards which have 2 factors in common and say why they are the same.

While the children are playing . . .

Does the child use a variety of categories for choosing bears or do they repeatedly use obvious ones, eg 'both brown', 'both big'?
Can the child explain confidently why a pair belongs together?

Both these bears have bow ties.

Teddy Allsorts

a game for 2–4 players

You will need

16 bear cards

How to play

1 Spread out all the bear cards on the table or carpet.

2 In your turn pick up two bears and say why they are alike. 'Both these bears have . . .'

3 If everyone agrees then you may keep the pair.

4 Carry on until all the cards have been picked up.

5 Count your cards. The winner is the person with most cards.